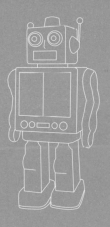

YOU KNOW YOU'RE A CHILD OF THE 1960s WHEN...

Charlie Ellis

summersdale

YOU KNOW YOU'RE A CHILD OF THE 1960s WHEN...

First published in 2006
Second edition published in 2010
This revised and updated edition copyright © Summersdale Publishers Ltd, 2016
Text by Mark Leigh, Mike Lepine and Vicky Edwards

Illustrations by Rita Kovács; icons © Shutterstock

Summersdale Publishers Ltd
46 West Street
Chichester
West Sussex
PO19 1RP
UK

www.summersdale.com

Printed and bound in China

ISBN: 978-1-84953-893-0

Substantial discounts on bulk quantities of Summersdale books are available to corporations, professional associations and other organisations. For details contact Nicky Douglas by telephone: +44 (0) 1243 756902, fax: +44 (0) 1243 786300 or email: nicky@summersdale.com.

To...

From...

YOU KNOW YOU'RE A CHILD OF THE 1960s WHEN...

Your lounge was pure **G Plan** and your kitchen boasted a pine breakfast bar.

Your most treasured possessions,
if you were a Mod, were your
ex-US army parka and
your Vespa...

Or, if you were a Rocker,
your leather jacket and
Triumph 500.

President John F. Kennedy

The president was shot and killed in Dallas, Texas, on 22 November 1963. Lee Harvey Oswald was arrested for the crime, but conspiracy theories surrounding the President's death sprang up around the time and persist to this day.

House Prices

In the 1960s the average house price in the UK was £2,530. Tower blocks – high-rise living – were constructed as an effective way of tackling the housing shortage caused by war damage and an increasing population. A symbol of the future back then, they're sadly considered a bit of an eyesore today.

SPACE EXPLORATION

One heck of a leap for mankind! The first space flight orbiting the Earth, man in space and later walking on the moon, and Luna 10 launched — it was all happening out there. Or *up* there.

YOU KNOW YOU'RE A CHILD OF THE 1960s WHEN...

You remember when driving on a motorway was a novelty rather than a necessary evil.

You moan that they don't
make things like they used to
(those fish knives you bought with
Green Shield Stamps in 1967 are
still going strong).

Lady Chatterley's Lover
was your generation's
Fifty Shades of Grey.

Although you have to sell
a kidney to fund your travel card
today, you remember the REAL
Great Train Robbery.

QUIZ

1. Which enduringly popular game, involving a mat and making your body as flexible as possible, was launched in this decade?

2. Which toy was created by British electronics engineer Denys Fisher, who invented it while researching a new design for bomb detonators for NATO?

3. Made in 1963 by the Pedigree Toys, which British doll was billed as 'the doll you love to dress'?

4 Which toy brand produced 16 different model cars in 1968?

5 Which late-1960s outdoor toy was allegedly inspired by a toy company director who spotted children bobbing about on a buoy in a Norwegian quay?

6 Launched in 1965 and still popular today, which game required being very steady-handed with a pair of tweezers?

7 Marketed for her ability to natter – a skill reflected in her name – what was this popular dolly called?

8 Originally described as 'a fully poseable artist's-dummy-style action figure', what was the Palitoy figure that went on to become a bestseller?

YOU KNOW YOU'RE
A CHILD OF THE
1960s
WHEN...

No kitchen purchase has ever given you a thrill to rival that of the Tupperware Square Seal Freezer Box.

Audrey Hepburn in *Breakfast at Tiffany's* remains the indisputable princess of chic. Fact.

You chuckle at the 'newfangled' trend for extensions and weaves – by the end of the 1960s, hair was everywhere; they even made a musical out of it.

The Beatles or The Rolling Stones? It's the original Blur vs Oasis!

Footy Matches

Going to a football match cost just 20p a ticket, so it was much more of an everyman's game than it is today. Decked out in your scarf and bobble hat set, hand-knitted in team colours, a loud but friendly yell in the stands followed by a bag of chips on the way home was the epitome of good, clean family fun.

Going to the Pictures

From the liveried commissionaire to the usherette with her torch and ice-cream tray, a trip to the pictures had a far greater sense of occasion about it. Plus, it was the most popular place to go if you wanted to hold hands or snog — that's what the back row was for, surely?

BUTLINS

Going to Butlins in the 1960s meant that
chalet living had never been so much
fun! Forget backpacking around Thailand
– knobbly knee and glamorous granny
competitions in Bognor Regis, Minehead
and Barry Island were the coolest ways
to spend your summer hols. Between
all the activities and the enthusiastic,
highly organised
Redcoats, you
barely even
had to
see your
family!

YOU KNOW YOU'RE
A CHILD OF THE
1960s
WHEN...

Double Diamond didn't
'work wonders', but you
drank it anyway.

Contributing home-made
Lipton Onion Soup Dip to the
church social buffet made you
the Nigella of your day.

You think that Twiggy makes
Kate and Cara look frumpy.

'Man on the moon' was
a moment in history, not a
Hollywood film.

QUIZ

ONLY A CHILD OF THE 1960s WILL KNOW...

Complete the titles of these 1960s TV shows:

1 *Dixon of...*

2 *Dr Finlay's...*

3 *Doctor in the...*

4 *Randall and...*

5 *Captain Scarlet and...*

6 Never Mind the Quality,...

7 A Man of Our...

8 Curry and...

YOU KNOW YOU'RE A CHILD OF THE 1960s WHEN...

You remember wearing skirts that were smaller than some of your current belts.

No matter how stylish the glossy mags claim that Sam Cam and Michelle Obama are, to you Jackie O is the godmother of glamour when it comes to political wives.

Fondue still feels like fine dining.

'Medicinal compound' is the intellectual property of Lily the Pink, not something you ask for over the counter in Boots.

Musical Heart-throbs

Elvis, John, Paul, George and Ringo, The Rolling Stones, Herman and his Hermits – there was no shortage of male pop pin-ups. As for the girls, Lulu, Cilla, Sandie Shaw and Dusty Springfield all set young male hearts a-flutter.

DJs

They were demigods – almost as beloved as the pop stars of the day. From 'Diddy' David Hamilton to Tony Prince, John Peel and of course the Togmeister himself, Sir Terry Wogan, these were heroes whose every word teenagers hung on.

Festivals

The main stage at Glasto? Pah! At the inaugural Isle of Wight Festival in 1968 two 40-foot trucks were the ONLY stage. Generally, festivals were smaller than the epic events of today, with jazz, folk and blues being the genres that dominated the scene.

The British Invasion

A golden decade for British music: The Beatles, The Who, The Rolling Stones, Cream, The Yardbirds, Donovan, Manfred Mann, The Kinks, Tom Jones and The Animals are just a few of the artists and bands who also made it big in the USA.

Brit Pop Pete

Smashing up his guitar and wearing Union Jack suits, Pete Townshend of The Who tapped into increasing teenage frustration, with 'My Generation' becoming an anthem of the time. From his experiments with distortion to his famous 'windmill' arm, he influenced decades of rock music.

YOU KNOW YOU'RE
A CHILD OF THE
1960s
WHEN...

You know that the Iron Curtain
cannot be found in IKEA.

You remember when
cigarettes came in solid,
rather than liquid, form.

You still know the lyrics of all the
songs in *The Sound of Music*.

The only female named Caroline
that really mattered was
that über-cool pirate radio
station ship.

QUIZ

ONLY A CHILD OF THE 1960s WILL KNOW...

1 Complete the title of the song: 'Strawberry Fields...'

2 In which Beatles song does Father McKenzie feature?

3 What was the hairstyle inspired by the Fab Four called?

4 In 1960 Paul McCartney and Pete Best were deported from Germany for nailing what to a bedroom wall and setting fire to it?

5 Who did John marry in 1962?

6 What are the Fab Four's surnames?

7 What was the original title of 'Yesterday'?

8 The Beatles attempted to adapt *The Lord of the Rings* for film, with George playing which role?

YOU KNOW YOU'RE A CHILD OF THE 1960s WHEN...

Pinky and Perky were so adorable that they almost put you off bacon butties.

Bingo was your mum's version of **Prosecco** and **pasta** with the girls.

Your loaf of choice was **Mother's Pride** and it only cost **five pence**.

You felt daring if you visited one of these newfangled supermarkets like **Mac Fisheries** or **Fine Fare**.

Wimpy Bars

The UK's answer to America's burger bars, Wimpy really began to take off. No cutlery required, food served within ten minutes of ordering and drinks served in a cardboard cup with a straw. Thrilling stuff.

Sweets

Spangles! Gobstoppers! Rainbow Crystals! Black Jacks! And a huge great bag of them for a shilling! (You'd get the money back when your teeth rotted, fell out and went under your pillow for the tooth fairy.)

PUDDINGS

Angel Delight (just add milk) launched, enabling the time-strapped housewife to simply whisk and serve. Other puds you may recall fondly include fruit in jelly (we served anything in jelly in the 1960s, even SPAM!) and pineapple upside-down cake.

YOU KNOW YOU'RE A CHILD OF THE 1960s WHEN...

Your mum did the laundry in
a twin tub using either
OMO or **Fairy Snow**.

You are well aware that
Noggin the Nog was a kids' TV
show and not a euphemism
for bedroom shenanigans.

You had to earn your pocket
money every week by cleaning
your dad's pride and joy:
his Mk I Cortina.

You took your holiday snaps with a
Kodak Instamatic, which felt like
cutting-edge technology.

QUIZ

ONLY A CHILD OF
THE 1960s WILL KNOW...

1 On what date did Neil Armstrong set foot on the Moon?

2 Which state was Woodstock held in?

3 The Kray twins were sentenced to life imprisonment at which famous courthouse?

4 What was the last underground line to be opened in the 1960s?

5 Which coin was issued on 14 October 1969?

6 The Concorde passenger jet was first displayed to the public at what show?

7 Which comedy team made their debut on TV on 5 October 1969?

8 Which singer returned his MBE in November 1969?

Answers 1. 20 July 1969 **2.** New York **3.** The Old Bailey **4.** Victoria **5.** 50p **6.** The Paris Air Show **7.** Monty Python **8.** John Lennon

35

YOU KNOW YOU'RE
A CHILD OF THE
1960s
WHEN...

You used to have
flowers in your hair.
Now it's Grecian 2000.

In any conversation about *The X Factor* you find yourself muttering about *Opportunity Knocks*.

You can still recall the names of all six firemen in Trumpton (OK, it's Pugh, Pugh, Barney McGrew, Cuthbert, Dibble and Grub).

You were repeatedly told to never trust 'The Man'. Too late, you found out that The Man in question is managing your pension fund.

Boutiques

London boutiques like Quorum, Bus Stop and Mary Quant's Bazaar were new and worth trekking to, wherever you lived. Just being able to say you had window-shopped at these 'emporiums of hip' made you fashion-forward. Biba was the pinnacle of affordable fashion, with girls everywhere falling in love with the strangely stiff Biba smock.

The London Look

'In New York it's the "London Look", in Paris it's "le style Anglais".' Described thus by *Vogue*, after years in the style doldrums, the UK was a major player in 1960s fashion. And we were swinging, baby!

GO-GO BOOTS

White, low-heeled and calf-length, the original Go-go boots were the perfect footwear to team with your Mary Quant mini and paved the way for boots that were a variation on a theme that continued into the next decade.

YOU KNOW YOU'RE A CHILD OF THE 1960s WHEN...

You still think of **Cuba**
as a base for **Soviet** missiles
and not a trendy package
holiday destination.

In your heart you're still a
free-spirited flower child –
albeit a free-spirited flower child
with a mortgage, 2.4 children and
a nine-to-five job in IT.

You used to call everybody
over 30 'Granddad'. It's not
so funny now, is it?

You used to really want to
marry that girl in the balloon
from the Nimble advert.
Her or Lady Penelope.

QUIZ

1. In which film did Nöel Coward play Mr Bridger?

2. What was the bear in the Disney film *The Jungle Book* called?

3. Complete the title: *Butch Cassidy and...*

4. In which 1964 musical film did Julie Andrews and Dick Van Dyke co-star?

5 Elizabeth Taylor starred as which historical beauty in 1963?

6 Which film starred Clint Eastwood and was set around a plot to find gold that had been buried in a remote cemetery?

7 What was the name of the film about a slave, featuring Kirk Douglas in the title role?

8 Whose baby was a 1968 film starring Mia Farrow?

YOU KNOW YOU'RE A CHILD OF THE 1960s WHEN...

Growing up as a girl, the only careers that were open to you involved typing, nursing or hairdressing.

You once looked to India for spiritual enlightenment, rather than banking enquiries and train times.

Your first boyfriend said you looked just like Cilla Black – and it was the ultimate compliment.

You remember when there were only three TV channels – and they were only on for part of the day... yet there was still more good stuff to watch than on the Sky TV bundle today.

Mod Mode

If you were a Mod then chances are that granny approved. With your Harrington jacket worn over your neat Fred Perry shirt, you cut a tidy dash.

Peacock Look

With your crushed velvet double-breasted suit or your brocade waistcoat, the foppish Edwardian style, popular in the mid and late 1960s, would have marked you out as a Peacock. Famous figures included the excellently named Savile Row tailor Tommy Nutter and Mick Jagger.

Tanked Up

Have you still got the knitted tank top, lovingly made by Aunty Maud, stashed at the back of a drawer? A popular sleeveless jumper – a sort of woolly vest you could wear over your shirt – this baby endured into the next decade.

Collar Cool

Nehru collars on shirts and jackets were upright, mandarin-style. When The Beatles and The Monkees were seen sporting these, demand shot through the roof and any self-respecting fashionable fella followed the collar revolution.

Denim

Jeans became popular as casual wear for chaps during the 1960s. Had a pair of Levi's or Wrangler jeans in your wardrobe? Well, you were a cat, and no mistake!

Chelsea Boots

You were bang on trend if you were shod with a pair of these – or at least some sort of ankle boots with a Cuban heel. You wore brogues for visiting your nana, of course, but boots, even if they gave you blisters, were your footwear of choice.

YOU KNOW YOU'RE A CHILD OF THE 1960s WHEN...

If you were a boy, you really, really wanted to be an **astronaut**. Or a **train driver**.

You always used to know where north was as a child – as long as you took off one of your Clarks Commandos shoes and peeked at the hidden compass inside.

You can reminisce for hours about Magilla Gorilla, Ivor the Engine and Topo Gigio.

Your birthday cards usually contained a ten-shilling note or a book token (and you were blimmin' grateful).

QUIZ

1. Who captained the 1966 England World Cup team?

2. Who was the 'Flying Scot' racing driver who recorded 27 race wins during his career?

3. Who 'floated like a butterfly'?

4. Who was known by the nickname of 'Golden Bear'?

5 Who won the Grand Slam, first as an amateur in 1962 and then as a pro in 1969?

6 How many major championships did 1960s golf star Arnold Palmer win during his career – five, six or seven?

7 Which swimmer was given a ten-year ban for horseplay during the 1964 Olympics, thus ending her career?

8 Danish Paul Elvstrøm was an Olympian in which sport?

YOU KNOW YOU'RE A CHILD OF THE 1960s WHEN...

You once thought **Cliff Richard** was a rock 'n' roll rebel – until he entered the **Eurovision Song Contest**.

You're still sensitive about wearing glasses in case people start calling you Joe 90.

You remember Nelson Mandela going to prison.

Every visit to the Saturday morning pictures at the ABC would be spoiled by some crap made by the Children's Film Foundation (usually about go-karting and starring Dennis Waterman).

Jackanory

The fantastic storytelling programme in which some of our finest actors would read a bit of a story each day; there was none of this instant gratification nonsense. If you wanted to find out what happened in the next chapter, you had to tune in again tomorrow.

Camberwick Green

Brian Cant was all over kids' TV like a rash in the 1960s. In *Camberwick Green* he provided the narration for the stop-motion puppet cast. The first in the Trumptonshire trilogy, *Camberwick Green* always started with a shot of a music box, which Cant would tease the audience with, asking us to guess what was in there today.

DOCTOR WHO

The TARDIS time tour began in 1963 with William Hartnell as the good Doctor. The first ever story was entitled 'An Unearthly Child' and a nation was quickly hooked. Nightmares about being chased by Daleks followed.

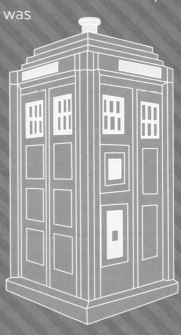

YOU KNOW YOU'RE A CHILD OF THE 1960s WHEN...

Your first pair of **Levi's** cost one pound, seventeen and six.

One of the TV shows you watched as a kid involved hapless hamsters and rats stuffed into miniature boats – and everyone found this very funny.

You sometimes wonder how you ever survived growing up in a world without airbags, seat belts or childproof medicine bottles.

You were never, ever convinced that the Milkybar Kid was 'strong and tough'.

QUIZ

ONLY A CHILD OF THE 1960s WILL KNOW...

1. What was the name given to traditionally long-haired people – many of whom settled in the Haight-Ashbury area of San Francisco in the mid 1960s – who rejected established society?

2. What was the word 'Mod' short for?

3. Which hairstyle was Brigitte Bardot famous for wearing?

4. Whose muse was socialite Edie Sedgwick?

5 Who brought hot pants and plastic macs to 1960s wardrobes?

6 Who wore the classic white bikini in the Bond film *Dr. No*?

7 Who posed nude for promotional shots for the smash-hit musical *Hair*?

8 What kind of dress did Audrey Hepburn make famous in *Breakfast at Tiffany's*?

YOU KNOW YOU'RE A CHILD OF THE 1960s WHEN...

Your bible used to be *On the Road.* (Now it's a Haynes manual for your Vauxhall Vectra.)

You've enjoyed one
summer of love – and over
20 summers of hosepipe bans.

You used to believe you'd be living
on the Moon by the twenty-first
century. (The Brooke Bond Tea
Cards lied.)

You had a mad granny who'd
gleefully give you a ha'penny
to go on holiday with and advise
you – in all seriousness – not to
spend it all at once.

This Is Your Life

Billed as a 'biographical television documentary' *This Is your Life* was more of a cross between an awards ceremony and a reality show. Eamonn Andrews would sneak up on celebs of the day and surprise them with his big red book, which was crammed with all their most embarrassing childhood photographs and messages from geriatric teachers.

Ready Steady Go!

RSG! (as it was affectionately known) was the first British pop music telly programme and went out on Friday evenings. Launched in 1963, the top pop acts of the day played live, including the Fab Four, who took the show's ratings when they appeared in March 1964.

THE AVENGERS

A much-loved spy series that was rich in wit and style, and had Dame Diana Rigg (the fantasy of men all over the country) romping about in a catsuit — this was telly in the 1960s at its very best. The lead character, John Steed, was impressive in his smart British gentleman uniform of suit, hat and umbrella.

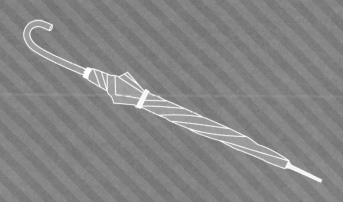

YOU KNOW YOU'RE A CHILD OF THE 1960s WHEN...

T.H.R.U.S.H. was the sworn enemy of the Man from U.N.C.L.E. – and not the subject of cringey telly adverts.

All it took to impress a girl was a **Babycham** followed by dinner at a **Berni Inn**.

You're secretly proud of your **Tufty Club** membership.

It once took trips to at least **eight different shops** to get all the weekly groceries.

QUIZ

1. Which product 'makes the most of a man'?

2. What car would you 'get away in'?

3. What was '57 times better'?

4. Fill in the product name: 'In the inch war, __ helps you win'.

5. What could help hands that do dishes feel as soft as your face?

6 What chocolate was 'sixpence worth of heaven'?

7 What product was advertised with the slogan: 'The happiest people you meet in the morning get their sunshine out of a box'?

8 Which brand was 'tea you can really taste'?

YOU KNOW YOU'RE A CHILD OF THE 1960s WHEN...

Your mum's kitchen radio
was perpetually tuned to
Sing Something Simple and
that blimmin' accordian.

You used to live in fear of the
four-minute warning; now it's
the feral kids off the local estate.

You have a vague memory
of a BBC comedy that starred
Terry Scott and Hugh Lloyd
as two garden gnomes...
or did you just imagine it?

The aerial of your dad's car had a
woolly tiger tail attached to it.

DO YOU REMEMBER...

Goldfinger

The third outing for Sean Connery as Bond, and with a very foxy Honor Blackman as Pussy Galore, this 1964 movie packed 'em in at the flicks. The first Bond film to win an Academy Award, it also managed to recoup its budget within two weeks of being on general release.

Alfie

Jude Law can just Do One. The REAL *Alfie* was of course Michael Caine in the original movie of 1966, which was adapted from the play and the novel of the same name. A romantic comedy about a cheeky chap with a penchant for the ladies, it was the first movie to carry a 'mature audiences' certificate.

Breakfast at Tiffany's

Frankly, Audrey Hepburn could have just stood there and we'd all have fallen in love with the movie, but the fact that the lady could actually act as well made

Breakfast at Tiffany's a hit that has become an absolute classic. All together now: 'Moon river...'

Psycho

The original American horror-slasher movie, Hitchcock scared the pants off us with his shocking but utterly gripping cinematic story. Fortunately, showers were pretty rare in 1960s Britain, or we might never have washed properly again.

The Graduate

Considered very naughty for its time, the idea of the young Dustin Hoffman copping off with his mother-in-law-to-be was simply jaw-slackening. Hoffman and Anne Bancroft gave sublime performances and the film is now regarded as iconic. Quite right too.

The Jungle Book

Inspired by Rudyard Kipling's famous story and released to critical acclaim in 1967, the film grossed over $73 million in the United States alone. The soundtrack has been one of Disney's most successful ever, with almost every song becoming a sing-along number for long car journeys.

YOU KNOW YOU'RE A CHILD OF THE 1960s WHEN...

You recall watching westerns where the goodies would wear white hats and the baddies would wear black hats – none of this moral ambiguity nonsense.

You blame sweet cigarettes and liquorice pipes for your current 60-a-day habit.

You remember when Carnaby Street attracted swinging cats, not gullible tourists.

Most of your toys came from Tri-ang, Matchbox or Chad Valley.

QUIZ

1. Who had a hit with 'My Old Man's a Dustman'?

2. Which singer and backing group asked 'Please Don't Tease'?

3. Whose clown did The Everly Brothers have a hit with?

4. Which singer and backing group assured us in song that we would 'never walk alone'?

5 Which group was 'Tired of Waiting for You'?

6 Who had a hit with 'Where do you go to My Lovely'?

7 Who sang about Blackberry Way?

8 What kind of woman did The Rolling Stones have a hit with in 1969?

YOU KNOW YOU'RE A CHILD OF THE 1960s WHEN...

The most exotic dishes you'd ever tasted were prawn cocktail and Black Forest Gateau.

You can still remember when British female tennis players were good (and plentiful).

The Pacemakers were a pop band who played with a bloke called Gerry – not essentials for your everyday living.

They used to tell you to 'go to work on an egg'. Bizarre advice – but these days an egg is still more likely to get you to work on time than South West Trains.

Vidal Sassoon

A British hairdresser with an exotic-sounding name, Sassoon created a brand new (and much copied) way of styling, favouring harsh, geometric cutting that eliminated the need for lacquer and looked the business. Most famous for creating the bob, for a long time Sassoon was THE name in hairdressing.

Yardley

In 1967 Twiggy became the face of Yardley, a company that had been established in 1770. Flogging Twiggy Eyelashes, Twiggy Paint and a range of other cosmetics, Yardley became symbolic of the new 'Swinging London' youth culture, rather than the bath salts and talcum powder for which it is probably better known today.

CLEOPATRA EYELINER FLICKS

Movies influenced style and trends hugely, and Elizabeth Taylor as Cleopatra became a look to emulate for girls and women of the time. It took time to perfect and you risked looking like a cross between a panda and an extra in *The Mikado* if you got it wrong.

YOU KNOW YOU'RE
A CHILD OF THE
1960s
WHEN...

The biggest dilemma in your life used to be whether to have a **Zoom** or **Skyray** lollipop.

The Loneliness of the Long Distance Runner spoke to you.

You really believed that
Nice Girls Don't.

It was a family tradition
to spend your evening in
front of *Corrie*.

QUIZ

ONLY A CHILD OF THE 1960s WILL KNOW...

1. Sydney Camm, Ralph Hooper and Stanley Hooker invented an aircraft. What was unique about it?

2. Peter Scott helped to found which nature-focussed charity?

3. Who invented the Marshall amplifier and speaker stack?

4. What was the name of the drug, pioneered by James Black, that successfully blocks

the heart's adrenaline-responsive beta-receptors?

5 Owen Maclaren designed the first lightweight what?

6 Frank Pantridge, a former World War Two medical officer, invented the portable what?

7 Which company marketed the CV-2000, the first home videotape recorder?

8 What kind of transplant operation first took place in 1967?

YOU KNOW YOU'RE A CHILD OF THE 1960s WHEN...

Your three favourite possessions were once a poster of **Che Guevara**, a **Donovan** album and a large orange **beanbag**.

You're solidly and defiantly pre-metric and still haven't got a clue about how long a kilo is or how heavy a centilitre might be.

You had your tonsils removed and woke up to ice cream rather than MRSA.

You still think John Lennon is the greatest person who ever lived – even after you found out about his penchant for urinating over nuns. Oh well, no one's perfect...

DO YOU REMEMBER...

The Teasmade

A creation that meant you would wake up half an hour before you needed to by dint of the noise that the damn thing made as it set about boiling and pouring; a cup of tea in bed may have been a novelty but it wasn't quite the invention of the future that we hoped.

Phillips E3300 Cassette Tape Recorder

The world's first cassette tape recorder, complete with a microphone so that you could record your own voice, the E3300 was another product that set you apart from the rest of the pack. Representing cutting-edge technology, and considered sleek and compact, it was also incredibly well made.

POLAROID SWINGER INSTANT CAMERA

What, no film to wrestle out and send away to be developed? What sort of witchcraft was this? Launched in 1966 in the UK, photos might only have been in black and white, but hey, so was the telly! The clunkier parent of the later colour model, the Swinger was added by hopeful teens to their birthday and Christmas lists.

YOU KNOW YOU'RE A CHILD OF THE 1960s WHEN...

You watched *Harry Potter and The Chamber of Secrets* and admired the *Ford Anglia 105E* far more than the plot.

You actually took the trouble to make your own **clothes**.

The first erotic photo you ever saw was of **Christine Keeler** sitting on a chair.

You were absolutely stunned that a contestant on *Double Your Money* could walk away with as much as £600.

QUIZ

ONLY A CHILD OF THE 1960s WILL KNOW...

1. Who did Princess Margaret marry in 1960?

2. Which of the Queen's children was born in 1960?

3. Prince Charles was invested as Prince of Wales in which year?

4. In which royal residence was Prince Andrew born?

5. The first film about Royal family life was

made in 1969. To the nearest million, how many people watched it?

6 How many Prime Ministers served the Queen during the 1960s?

7 Which of the Queen's children joined Benenden School, in Kent, in 1963?

8 Who was born on 1 July 1961 at Park House near Sandringham, Norfolk?

YOU KNOW YOU'RE A CHILD OF THE 1960s WHEN...

You can remember lava lamps, parkas and the Mini...
the first time round.

You recall the thrill of reading *Janet and John* – and being desperate to find out what happened when they went through the garden gate...

You haven't quite given up the dream of your future career being 'suave super spy'.

Your parents threatened to throw you out if you ever became a hippy.

Austin Mini

Created by Sir Alec Issigonis, the Mini was launched in 1959. Distinctive and diminutive, this baby characterises the 1960s more than any other car and is arguably the star of the movie *The Italian Job*, upstaging a cast that included Michael Caine and Nöel Coward.

Fiat 124

Another popular little car (European Car of the Year in 1967), the 124 was heralded for its advanced coil suspension and all round disc brakes. Its design and tooling were ultimately bought by the Russians, who transformed it into... the Lada. *Mio Dio!*

E-Type Jaguar Roadster

Off the back of Jaguar's racing success the previous decade, the E-Type caused a rumpus when she first appeared at the Geneva Motor Show in 1961. Trumping all other cars in its genre, the Roadster was also extremely competitively priced.

Ford Zephyr

Not a great deal going for it: the Zephyr was slow, handled badly and there was nothing attractive about its appearance. Oddly, it remained popular as a getaway car by villains of the decade. Maybe the baddies knew something that we didn't?

Rover P6 2000

Launched in 1963, the P6 2000 took the world by storm. Boasting an overhead cam engine, all round disc brakes and an exciting new shape, this was the first compact executive saloon car. Bank managers everywhere lusted after it.

Mk I Cortina

Advertised by Ford as the small car with a big difference, the Mark 1 was terrific value. Stylish too, it even appeared in *Carry On Cabby*!

YOU KNOW YOU'RE A CHILD OF THE 1960s WHEN...

Patience wasn't just a virtue: it was a necessity when TV sets took five minutes to warm up.

You can still remember not only how to dance the Twist, but also the Hitch-Hike, the Watusi, the Chicken and the Mashed Potato.

You learned the facts of life from playground rumours and your older brother's copy of *Health and Efficiency*.

The opening sequences to *Mission: Impossible* and *The Banana Splits* are indelibly stamped on your brain.

QUIZ

ONLY A CHILD OF THE 1960s WILL KNOW...

1. Which matinee idol, dubbed 'King of Hollywood' died in 1960?

2. Which rock 'n' roll pioneer died in a car crash in 1960?

3. Which Nobel prize-winning author died in July 1961?

4. Which actress was found dead in her Hollywood bungalow on 5 August 1962?

5 Which British World War Two leader died in 1965?

6 Which American author and poet was found dead on 11 February 1963?

7 Which founding member of The Rolling Stones drowned in 1969?

8 Which star of *The Wizard of Oz* died on 22 June 1969?

YOU KNOW YOU'RE A CHILD OF THE 1960s WHEN...

You remember George Best more for hitting the back of the net than hitting the bottle.

You'd happily occupy yourself for hours with a packet of pipe cleaners, paper clips and some cereal boxes, trying to create some totally useless item like they made on *Blue Peter*.

Walking home from school was relatively safe; no one ever got mugged for their new plimsolls.

Your first crush was the boy at the funfair who took the money on the Waltzer.

DO YOU REMEMBER...

'Cool!'

Originally a 1950s slang word, it became the most used word of the 1960s.

'Libber'

Someone who supports the women's movement. Second-wave feminism was pouring over from the US and suddenly equality issues that had been buried in the post-war 1950s were a big topic of conversation.

'PSYCHEDELIC'

Enlightenment of any kind that was achieved in a less than conventional way; trippy culture trickled into fashion, art and music.

YOU KNOW YOU'RE A CHILD OF THE 1960s WHEN...

You know the difference between Mr Spock and Dr Spock.

The biggest playground status symbol was owning a 'Johnny Seven' (seven guns in one!).

You remember your granny getting strangely excited when Jackie Pallo turned up on the wrestling.

You got all your funniest lines from Ken Dodd.

ONLY A CHILD OF
THE 1960s WILL KNOW...

1. Which guitarist left Sidcup art school in the early 1960s to concentrate on music, going on to be named as one of *Rolling Stone* magazine's greatest guitarists of all time?

2. In which London street can you find a blue plaque marking the house in which Jimi Hendrix was born?

3. Who made the classic 1960s album *The 'Twangs' the 'Thang'*?

4 What type of guitar did Hendrix play on his *Are You Experienced* album?

5 Ronnie Wood and Rod Stewart left what group in 1969 to join the Small Faces?

6 John Fogerty was lead singer and guitarist with which 1960s band?

7 Who was the drummer in The Who?

8 Whose debut album, released in 1968, was called *Truth*?

YOU KNOW YOU'RE
A CHILD OF THE
1960s
WHEN...

DI Barlow was the dirtiest, meanest cop you'd ever seen on TV.

Being caned or having a blackboard rubber thrown at your head was a perfectly acceptable part of school life, not a precursor to your teacher being suspended and splashed all over *The Mail on Sunday*.

Your John Collier charge card marked you out as a high roller.

Playing conkers was more popular than playing truant.

Boxing

Thanks to a young chap called Cassius Clay, who changed his name to Muhammad Ali, boxing enjoyed a surge in interest in the 1960s, with clubs attracting many youngsters who wanted to put on their gloves and get stuck in.

Wrestling

When the TV show *World of Sport* launched in the middle of the decade, it brought wrestling into our front parlours on Saturday afternoons and made stars of the chunky chaps who threw themselves about the ring. Camp, theatrical and regarded as family-friendly, elderly ladies, it seemed, were especially fond of wrestling as a spectator sport.

THE WORLD CUP

One of the most glorious moments of English football came in 1966 when England won the World Cup. The ONLY TIME England has won the World Cup, we can still recite every member of the victorious team from memory (even though we've forgotten other things).

YOU KNOW YOU'RE A CHILD OF THE 1960s WHEN...

You bought all your singles from Boots the Chemist.

The three most significant letters in your life used to be CND. Now it's RSI.

You were entertained by the adventures of a bush kangaroo, even though it was really just Lassie with a pouch.

You still remember a thrilling sense of anticipation when watching *Grandstand's* teleprinter displaying the latest football results.

QUIZ

ONLY A CHILD OF
THE 1960s WILL KNOW...

1. Which Kennedy announced that he was to run for President in 1960?

2. Who was named the third chairman of the Palestine Liberation Organisation (PLO) in 1964?

3. Which Russian ballet dancer defected to the West?

4. Who became British Prime Minister in 1964?

5 Which communist country was famous for its Red Guards?

6 Who gave the famous 'I have a dream' speech?

7 Nikita Khrushchev was head of which state union?

8 Across which European capital was a wall erected?

YOU KNOW YOU'RE
A CHILD OF THE
1960s
WHEN...

You used to have really long hair
– just not growing out of
your nose and ears.

The answer was 'blowing in the wind' – not 42.

You remember a time before retro.

Your Sundays were once spent at a 'happening' and not a car boot sale.

19

The bible for fashion-conscious young women, this magazine was what you read to avoid making style blunders and ensuring that your wardrobe was always bang up to date — a favourite with secretaries whose biggest worry in life was whether or not their hemline was where it should be.

Beat Instrumental

For the serious 1960s pop and music fan, this was a magazine featuring far less frivolous gossip and much more analysis of the music. A bit dull, you bought it if you were a nerd or you wanted to impress.

Beatles Monthly

Published in the 1960s as a small format fan magazine, you couldn't consider yourself a proper groupie unless you subscribed to this publication. And you read it from cover to cover.

Commando War Stories in Pictures (Commando)

A comic series that was launched by D.C. Thomson of Dundee in 1961, in addition to their comics, such as *The Beano* and *The Dandy*. Demand quickly saw the publication doubling its issues to four per month. Boys big and small got their rocks off.

Rave

Super-trendy music magazine, its main selling point was loads of colour photographs of the stars of the day. A sort of *Smash Hits* grandpa.

Good Housekeeping

Still going strong today, in the 1960s no self-respecting housewife would miss her monthly.

YOU KNOW YOU'RE A CHILD OF THE 1960s WHEN...

After all these years you still can't fathom what that last episode of *The Prisoner* was all about.

You can't walk over
Waterloo Bridge without
thinking of Terry and Julie.

You still wonder what was
so wrong with John Tracy
that **International Rescue**
deliberately kept him up in space
alone on **Thunderbird Five** all
the time. (Body odour? Unnatural
interest in Grandma Tracy?)

You still know all the words to the
theme song of *Casey Jones*
('... a-steamin' and a-rollin'...').

QUIZ

1 Whose lover was subject to a book-based court case?

2 Who wrote the classic *To Kill a Mocking Bird*?

3 Complete the title of Anthony Burgess's book: *A Clockwork _*?

4 Who wrote *Catch-22*?

5 Which sweet-sounding Roald Dahl children's book was published in 1964?

6 Which Muriel Spark classic was published in 1961?

7 Who was the author of *2001: A Space Odyssey*?

8 Who was the author of *In Cold Blood*?

YOU KNOW YOU'RE A CHILD OF THE 1960s WHEN...

You would **knock** on your friend's door to see if they could come and play, not send them a **text message**.

If you wanted to watch something on TV, you probably had to go round your neighbour's house to see it.

Outdoor toilets were often a fact of life.

You were forced to wear short trousers to school regardless of the ambient temperature. Brrr!

The Beatles

Of course you do! The Beatles dominated the album chart, as well as the singles chart (no less than ten albums made it into the Top 20), but their most iconic album cover has to be *Sgt. Pepper's Lonely Hearts Club Band* (1967). A corker!

Simon and Garfunkel

More folky, Simon and Garfunkel were also pretty prolific in the 1960s, scoring three Top 20 albums. The duo's *Sounds of Silence* (1966) was undeniably a beaut. Even if Art's hair was scary.

THE ROLLING STONES

The *Rolling Stones No. 2* of 1965 was trounced by The Beatles, but still made it into the chart. And like they cared. When you were as cool as Mick and the boys, you had your own rating system. Mostly as notches on your bedpost.

If you're interested in finding out more
about our books, find us on Facebook at
Summersdale Publishers and follow us on
Twitter at **@Summersdale**.

www.summersdale.com